I0017546

REDMI NOTE 12 PRO 5G USER GUIDE

The Most Comprehensive Setup Secret Manual for Beginners and Seniors In Unleashing The Power Of Note 12 PRO 5G.

Felix S. Shearer

Copyright 2023, Felix S. Shearer

TABLE OF CONTENTS

1. Introduction

Getting Started with Redmi Note 12 PRO 5G

The Redmi Note 12 Pro 5G, which combines state-of-the-art capabilities with affordability, is a monument to the unrelenting advancement of smartphone technology. Here, we take a closer look at this amazing device, going over its features, design, and the first things users do after opening the package and configuring it.

Overview of the Mobile Device

The flagship product from Redmi, a well-known player in the smartphone industry, is the Redmi Note 12 Pro 5G.

It was released in 2023 and represents the newest developments in mobile technology, appealing to consumers looking for a robust but reasonably priced gadget. The smartphone has an elegant, contemporary appearance and a 6.67-inch AMOLED screen that produces clear, vivid images.

The MediaTek Dimensity 1080 CPU underpins the Redmi Note 12 Pro 5G, guaranteeing a smooth and snappy user experience. With 5G connectivity, the gadget is at the vanguard of the mobile data revolution and can download and upload data more quickly for a better online experience.

The gadget has a large 5000mAh battery, which is indicative of Redmi's dedication to offering long-lasting battery life. It stands out for its incredible 67 Watt fast charger, which allows customers to fully charge their device in just 40 minutes. One of the most frequent worries among smartphone users is the necessity for rapid and effective charging, which is addressed by this function.

Packaging and First Configuration

The moment you open the Redmi Note 12 Pro 5G after purchasing it sets the tone for your future experiences.

The smartphone itself, a USB Type-C cable, a 67 Watt fast charger, a user handbook, and a SIM card ejector tool are usually included in the packaging. Depending on the area and promotional offers, the gadget can additionally include supplementary accessories or promotional materials.

The initial setup procedure is intended to be simple and easy for consumers to navigate. The vivid AMOLED display welcomes users and walks them through the setup wizard upon turning on the device. A smooth integration of the device into the user's digital ecosystem is ensured by a number of preliminary procedures, including language selection, Wi-Fi connection, and Google account login.

Redmi places a strong emphasis on user customisation right out of the box, letting users customize their setup by adding themes, wallpapers, and app layouts to their device. This dedication to customization is also shown in the home screen, where users can arrange shortcuts and widgets to create a customized interface.

Users are presented with an array of biometric identification options by means of integrated security features, including fingerprint recognition and facial unlock, throughout the setup process. This offers a layer of convenience for consumers who want quick and safe access to their cellphones, while also improving device security.

The setup procedure for the Redmi Note 12 Pro 5G also helps users create and restore backups, making sure that important information and preferences are kept safe while switching to a new smartphone. Redmi's grasp of how important it is for users to have a smooth and stress-free onboarding experience is evident in this attention to detail.

Users are presented with the device's home screen, which highlights the vibrant display and the variety of pre-installed apps, after the first setup is finished. A clutter-free user interface is highly valued on Redmi, which offers a simple and easy-to-use layout that prioritizes important functionality above bloatware.

In summary, the launch and setup procedure of the Redmi Note 12 Pro 5G demonstrates a tasteful fusion of cutting-edge technology and user-focused design.

Redmi has created an experience that appeals to both tech enthusiasts and regular consumers, from the elegant design to the quick and easy initial setup, laying the groundwork for an engaging smartphone journey.

2. How to Use

Starting out with your Redmi Note 12 Pro 5G requires that you grasp the essentials of getting started. From turning on and off the smartphone to investigating the many unlocking techniques and simple navigation motions that characterize the user experience, this section walks users through all the necessary processes.

Switching the Device On or Off

Users can easily access their device with the Redmi Note 12 Pro 5G because turning it on is a simple process. The power button, which is usually found on the right side of the gadget, opens the door to a world of features and connectivity.

To begin the startup routine, just press and hold the power button for a few seconds. Then, the brilliant AMOLED display will display the Redmi logo.

On the other hand, shutting off the gadget is equally straightforward. Pressing and holding the power button displays a menu with the ability to restart or turn off the device. With a single tap of the screen, users can confirm their selection after selecting the desired option. This uncomplicated strategy fits with Redmi's dedication to offering an approachable and user-friendly experience.

Opening Techniques

A range of unlocking techniques are available for the Redmi Note 12 Pro 5G, accommodating customers' varying preferences for simplicity and security. Among the principal techniques are:

1. Fingerprint Recognition: With a rapid and secure touch, users can unlock their cell phones thanks to the fingerprint sensor, which is strategically placed on the device. Users register their fingerprints during the initial setup process, which generates a biometric key for easy authentication. The fingerprint recognition's quickness and precision add to the unlocking process' ease and speed.

2. Facial Unlock: The Redmi Note 12 Pro 5G uses facial recognition technology to let consumers unlock their devices with just a quick glance. Users take a facial scan to create a customized facial profile during the setup procedure. This technique improves the user experience by combining security and the ease of hands-free unlocking.

3. PIN and Password: The smartphone supports password- and PIN-based unlocking for consumers who prefer more conventional approaches. In the setup procedure, customers can choose to choose an alphanumeric password or a numeric PIN, which offers a familiar and secure alternative.

Redmi's commitment to providing choice and flexibility is reflected in the provision of numerous unlocking methods, acknowledging that consumers have varying preferences when it comes to striking a balance between security and convenience.

Guidance and Motions

With its simple gestures and controls, navigating the Redmi Note 12 Pro 5G's interface is a smooth experience. The gadget has an easy-to-use touch screen that responds to movements and improves user interaction. Important components of navigation include:

1. Home Screen Navigation: Users may swipe left or right to move between home screens, making a variety of apps and widgets easily accessible. Users can customize their experience by adding widgets, changing backgrounds, and arranging app icons to suit their tastes by long-pressing the home screen.

2. App Drawer: For organized access to installed apps, the Redmi Note 12 Pro 5G features an app drawer. The app drawer, which shows an extensive list of apps, may be accessed by swiping up from the home screen. This design decision streamlines the user experience by keeping the home screen clutter-free.

3. Notification Bar and Control Center: Users may check notifications quickly by swiping down from the top of the screen to expose the notification bar.

Furthermore, the control center, which offers instant access to crucial settings like Wi-Fi, Bluetooth, and screen brightness, can be accessed by swiping down from the right side.

4. Multitasking Gestures: With multitasking gestures, users may quickly navigate between open programs. One may effortlessly multitask and quickly move between apps by swiping up from the bottom and holding down the recent apps display.

To sum up, the Redmi Note 12 Pro 5G's focus on intuitive navigation and a variety of unlocking techniques add to a comprehensive and fulfilling user experience.

Users may easily engage with their smartphones by using intuitive motions to navigate through apps or unlock the device with a fingerprint touch, which creates a delightful and seamless digital experience.

3. Navigation and Interface

The Redmi Note 12 Pro 5G's navigation and interface play a crucial role in determining how the user feels overall. This part delves further into the nuances of the device's interface, examining the Home Screen, App Drawer, Notification Bar, and Control Center?essential components that shape users' daily interactions with their smartphones.

Home Screen: A Customized Center

The Redmi Note 12 Pro 5G's Home Screen, which gives users a customized canvas to express their preferences and expedite access to commonly used apps and services, is the entry point to the device's functionality.

- Organization and Customization: The home screen of the smartphone offers a recognizable grid arrangement in which users may customize the order of shortcuts, widgets, and app icons to fit their needs. Redmi places a strong emphasis on customization, enabling users to install widgets, change the wallpaper, and rearrange the iconography by long-pressing the home screen.

- Widgets and Dynamic Content: The Redmi Note 12 Pro 5G allows users to install a wide range of widgets to their home screens, which offer instant access to key features and information at a glance.

Users can customize their home screens to fit their needs, whether it's a calendar widget showing forthcoming activities or a weather widget providing real-time forecasts.

- **Swipe-Up App Suggestions:** Based on usage trends, app suggestions are revealed with a simple swipe up motion from the bottom of the home screen, further enhancing convenience. This clever feature provides a quick and easy method to access frequently used applications by predicting the apps users are likely to need.

- **Folder Organization:** The Redmi Note 12 Pro 5G allows users to create folders on the home screen, which is ideal for those who like to work in a more ordered manner.

Apps can be categorized and grouped together to simplify navigation and clear up the home screen.

App Drawer: Condensed Access to Applications

The Redmi Note 12 Pro 5G's App Drawer helps maintain a tidy and well-organized user interface so users can easily access the installed apps.

- **Swipe-Up Gesture:** Users can access the App Drawer, which shows a complete list of all installed apps, by swiping up from the home screen. This design decision simplifies program access and improves the visual cleanliness of the home screen, especially for customers who have a lot of installed applications.

- **Alphabetic Sorting and Search Function:** Finding specific programs is made easier because the App Drawer is frequently arranged alphabetically. Furthermore, a search feature saves time and facilitates hassle-free navigation by enabling users to easily identify and launch apps by inputting the app's name.

- **App Categories:** The Redmi Note 12 Pro 5G has the ability to classify apps in the App Drawer by organizing them according to their features or usage habits. This classification helps users find apps more quickly, which is especially helpful when there are a variety of apps available.

Control Center and Notification Bar: Easy Access to Preferences

The Redmi Note 12 Pro 5G's Notification Bar and Control Center, which provide users with easy access to notifications and commonly used settings, are crucial parts of the UI.

-      **Notification Bar:** To access the Notification Bar, slide down from the top of the screen. Incoming alerts and notifications are displayed there. With only a swipe, users can quickly dismiss notifications, and a handy clear-all option guarantees a notification-free experience.

- **Control Center:** Swiping down from the right side of the screen brings up the Control

Center, providing quick access to important settings. Users can adjust screen brightness, Wi-Fi, Bluetooth, and other options here. Efficiency is emphasized in the Control Center's architecture, which lets users change settings without having to go through several menus.

- **Customizable Quick Settings:** Users of the Redmi Note 12 Pro 5G can frequently rearrange toggles and prioritize them according to their own preferences by customizing the Quick Settings in the Control Center. This degree of personalization improves the user's capacity to adapt the interface to their own requirements.

- Notifications and App Shortcuts: The Control Center and Notification Bar may also offer shortcuts to frequently used programs and settings. This thoughtful integration reduces the need to switch between panels, making the experience more efficient and intuitive.

In summary, user ease and customization were prioritized in the design of the Redmi Note 12 Pro 5G's interface and navigation functions. Redmi has designed an interface that strikes a mix between usability and style, offering consumers a unified and simple platform for their everyday digital interactions. This includes features like the customizable home screen, the streamlined App Drawer, the quick-access Notification Bar, and Control Center.

4. Personalizing Your Device

Along with its impressive feature set, the Redmi Note 12 Pro 5G offers a plethora of customization options that let users personalize their device to fit their own preferences and style.

In this section, we delve into the art of customization on the Redmi Note 12 Pro 5G, covering things like adding custom themes and wallpapers, using widgets to organize the app layout, and skillfully controlling the home screen to create a customized user experience.

Customizing Wallpapers and Themes: Adding Style to Everything

The Redmi Note 12 Pro 5G's support for customisable themes and wallpapers is one of its best features; it lets users change the appearance and feel of their device with a few taps.

Theme Selection and Use: Redmi provides a wide variety of themes, each of which showcases a distinct visual aesthetic. The Themes app allows users to browse and select from a wide range of themes, from colorful and lively to sophisticated and minimalist.

Applying a theme results in an instant makeover, changing the device's color schemes, icons, and general appearance.

Wallpaper Customization: Having the option to choose your own wallpapers is more than just a decorative touch; it's a way for you to express yourself. For a more customized look, customers of the Redmi Note 12 Pro 5G can utilize their own photos or pick from a variety of preloaded wallpapers. Users are able to customize their wallpaper to express their individuality and mood, whether it be landscape photos, artwork, or a favorite picture.

Dynamic Themes and Live Wallpapers: Redmi frequently incorporates dynamic themes and live wallpapers to offer an additional degree of vibrancy. These components react to user input by subtly animating or altering their appearance according to the time of day, for example. The device feels more alive and responsive due to its dynamic nature, which also improves the entire user experience.

App Layout and Widgets: Customizing Features to Meet Your Requirements

The Redmi Note 12 Pro 5G's approach to widgets and app layout gives consumers a customizable canvas to effectively arrange their digital area.

Customizable App Layout and Icons: Users are free to reorganize their app icons to best fit their usage styles. Grid and list views are commonly supported by the Redmi Note 12 Pro 5G, giving users the option to select a layout that best suits their organizational needs. For individuals who like their home screen to be neat and organized, this flexibility is essential.

Widgets for Fast Access: Without opening the entire program, widgets act as dynamic shortcuts to particular app features, giving users rapid access to pertinent data. The Redmi Note 12 Pro 5G frequently supports a wide range of widgets, including calendar, music player, and weather widgets.

By long-pressing and choosing the relevant widget from the menu, users can add widgets to their home screens, improving the functionality of the device with information that is easily accessed.

Smart App Organization Suggestions: Based on usage trends, the device might also come with intelligent app organization suggestions. This feature makes the process of organizing an app easier by making recommendations for folders or classifications based on the user's preferences. For a hassle-free app organization experience, users can decide to adopt these recommendations.

Overseeing the Home Screen: A Harmony of Structure and Usability

The home screen serves as the main interface for user interaction with the Redmi Note 12 Pro 5G, and it places a great deal of control in the hands of the user to manage this important area.

Creating Folders for Organization: The Redmi Note 12 Pro 5G has the ability to create folders on the home screen, which enables users to organize apps based on similarities. With only a few clicks, users may create folders to arrange their programs in a way that facilitates easier navigation. This is a very useful feature for customers that have a large software library.

Removing and Rearranging Apps: Redmi makes sure customers are in complete control of the apps that are available on their home screen. By long-pressing and dragging an app to the desired location, you may quickly rearrange it. Likewise, unneeded apps may be quickly removed by choosing the uninstall option, which helps maintain a clean home screen.

Easy Access to Features and Settings: The Redmi Note 12 Pro 5G frequently includes on-screen shortcuts to frequently used settings. Features like Wi-Fi, Bluetooth, and screen brightness can be included in these shortcuts.

Users no longer have to go through menus to access frequently used settings because these shortcuts are conveniently located on the home screen.

Backup and Restore Options: The Redmi Note 12 Pro 5G frequently comes with backup and restore options for home screen layouts, understanding how important it is to have a smooth transition between devices. By guaranteeing that customers may maintain their meticulously designed home screen configuration when updating or transferring devices, this reduces the work needed to replicate their favored arrangement.

Result: An Instrument as Special as You Are

In summary, the Redmi Note 12 Pro 5G is distinguished not just by its potent specs but also by its dedication to user customization. Redmi has created a smartphone that can be customized to the user's tastes, from themes and wallpapers that change the device's visual identity to widgets and app layouts that improve functionality.

The user's sense of control and ownership is further reinforced by the ability to easily rearrange apps, manage the home screen with folders, and access settings. The Redmi Note 12 Pro 5G is a canvas for personal expression, making every user's device as distinct as they are. It's more than simply a smartphone.

5. Calling and Receiving

A Smooth Communication Experience

The Redmi Note 12 Pro 5G stands out in the crowded smartphone market not just for its cutting-edge features but also for its effective and user-friendly calling capabilities. The user experience of placing and taking calls on the device is examined in this section, along with the other call capabilities that improve communication in general. Dialing, answering, and ending calls are all covered in detail.

Making Calls: A Quick and Easy Procedure

Redmi Note 12 Pro 5G makes calling easier and faster, allowing users to communicate with others quickly and conveniently.

Phone App Interface: The Phone app, which serves as a central hub for all calling-related operations, is usually where the calling experience starts. Redmi makes sure that the user interface is easy to understand by providing a contact list for perusing saved contacts, a call log for instant access to recent calls, and a numeric keypad for manual dialing.

Manual Dialing: The numeric keypad allows users to manually dial phone numbers if they would rather use the more conventional approach. The Redmi Note 12 Pro 5G guarantees responsiveness by precisely registering every press. Predictive text is one example of a smart feature that can speed up contact location search based on partial number or name inputs.

Integration of Contact List: Redmi smoothly incorporates the contact list into the dialing procedure. With only one swipe, users may navigate through their contacts, select the required entry, and start a call. This integration reduces the possibility of calling errors while simultaneously improving convenience.

Voice Recognition: Using voice instructions, users can start calls on some devices that have voice recognition technology installed. Voice recognition on the Redmi Note 12 Pro 5G adds a level of hands-free simplicity that is particularly useful for consumers who are constantly on the go.

Taking and Hanging Up Calls: Simple and Intuitive Mechanisms

With its simple controls and intuitive design, the Redmi Note 12 Pro 5G makes sure that making and ending calls is a simple chore for users.

Incoming Call Interface: The gadget shows the incoming call interface when a call comes in.

The name or phone number of the caller is usually displayed on this interface, along with the ability to accept or reject the call. Redmi's design prioritizes efficiency and clarity, providing consumers with information and icons that are instantly recognized.

Taking Calls: Users can swipe the screen or press the dedicated answer button to take up an incoming call. The time between answering the call and establishing a connection is reduced thanks to this gesture-based method, which guarantees a prompt response. To improve accessibility, users might also be able to take calls right from the lock screen.

Ending Calls: With the Redmi Note 12 Pro 5G, ending a call is as easy as touching the button or making a motion, like swiping down on the screen. The call is quickly ended by the device, which then takes consumers back to their original screen or the call log.

Quick Decline Options: Redmi frequently offers the ability to quickly decline incoming calls. Sending a pre-written message is one of these choices, allowing users to indicate that they are unavailable without actually taking the call. This functionality takes care of circumstances in which it would not be convenient to answer the call.

Features of the Call: Enhancing the Interaction Experience

In addition to the basic functions of placing and receiving calls, the Redmi Note 12 Pro 5G offers a number of features that improve communication in general and meet a variety of user requirements.

Call Waiting and Holding: Call waiting is a feature that Redmi normally offers, enabling customers to take an incoming call while on a previous call. To ensure they have control over many calls at once, users can decide whether to answer the second call or put the first one on hold.

Conference Calls: The Redmi Note 12 Pro 5G frequently supports conference calls for customers who are participating in group or collaborative talks. By allowing users to add more people to a single call, this feature promotes effective communication and does away with the necessity for separate chats.

Call Recording: Redmi acknowledges the value of call recording for a number of reasons, such as meeting regulatory requirements or retaining crucial information. A built-in call recording function of the gadget might enable users to record calls with only a tap.

Voicemail Integration: The voicemail feature of the Redmi Note 12 Pro 5G is smoothly integrated into the calling experience.

The Phone app offers users the ability to access and manage voicemail straight from the app, providing a single destination for all communication-related tasks.

Caller ID and Spam Protection: Redmi often has sophisticated Caller ID features that tell users of the caller's background. The gadget might also have spam prevention features that alert users to potentially fraudulent or spammy calls and identify them, shielding them from interruptions that they don't want.

Final Thought: Redefining the Dynamics of Communication

To sum up, the Redmi Note 12 Pro 5G aims to change communication dynamics for customers by using a unique method to make and receive calls. With features that accommodate a range of user preferences, the gadget makes sure that making calls is both efficient and intuitive.

The Redmi Note 12 Pro 5G prioritizes the user experience, from the quick and efficient calling procedure to the simple controls for taking and ending calls. The addition of sophisticated call functions raises the smartphone's profile even further by providing a feature-rich and user-friendly communication interface.

6. Messaging and Communication

Beyond its ability to make and receive calls and connect to the internet, the Redmi Note 12 Pro 5G shines at offering a smooth and comprehensive messaging and communication experience.

In this section, we look at how the smartphone makes texting easier, uses messaging apps to meet a variety of communication needs, and connects social media and email to keep users in constant contact.

Texting: A Time-Honored, Trusted Approach

Text messaging is still the mainstay of mobile communication, and the Redmi Note 12 Pro 5G makes sure that this essential function is both feature-rich and easy to use.

Built-in Messaging App: A built-in messaging app that provides a simple text message sending and receiving interface is usually pre-installed on the device. Redmi makes sure that this software is efficient and makes it easy for users to compose and send messages.

Text Input Methods: The Redmi Note 12 Pro 5G facilitates many text input methods, such as voice input and a snappy virtual keyboard.

Predictive text recommendations are frequently included in virtual keyboards, which speed up typing and reduce errors. Users can dictate texts with voice input, which is convenient.

Multimedia Messaging (MMS): The Redmi Note 12 Pro 5G offers Multimedia Messaging Service (MMS), which allows users to send and receive multimedia assets via text messages, including photographs, videos, and audio files. This goes beyond standard text messaging. The expressive power of messages is enhanced by this feature.

Delivery and Read Receipts: Redmi frequently integrates these features into its messaging application.

These indicators let users know when their message has been successfully viewed by the receiver and when it has been delivered to their device. The dynamics of communication are improved by this transparency, particularly when there is a deadline involved.

Messaging Apps: Various Choices for Different Needs

To accommodate a range of communication demands and preferences, the Redmi Note 12 Pro 5G supports a multitude of messaging apps in addition to standard text messaging.

Well-known Messaging Apps: Generally, the gadget is compatible with well-known messaging apps such as

Telegram, WhatsApp, and Signal, giving users the freedom to select the one that best suits their communication style and social networks. Additional capabilities like group conversations, multimedia sharing, and audio and video calls are frequently offered by these programs.

Unified Messaging Hub: The Redmi Note 12 Pro 5G frequently incorporates messaging applications into a unified messaging hub, giving consumers a single area to handle interactions on several platforms. The user experience is streamlined by this connection, which does away with the need to switch between programs.

Security and Privacy Features: The Redmi Note 12 Pro 5G may include features like end-to-end encryption in compatible messaging apps since it understands how important security is when it comes to texting. This increases user confidence in digital communication by guaranteeing that interactions stay private and safe.

Social Media and Email: Integrated Connectivity

The Redmi Note 12 Pro 5G's ability to communicate goes beyond texting because it easily incorporates social media and email.

Email Integration: A specialized email app is usually included with the device, enabling users to set up and maintain their email accounts from their cellphones.

Redmi makes sure that this software has an intuitive user interface so that users can compose, send, and receive emails with ease.

Push Notifications: The Redmi Note 12 Pro 5G enabled push notifications for emails in order to notify users as soon as possible. When fresh emails come, users are notified instantly, which improves email communication's responsiveness. Users may also be able to personalize the device's notification settings for every email account.

Social Media Apps: Facebook, Instagram, Twitter, and other social media sites are easily integrated into the Redmi Note 12 Pro 5G through the use of specialized apps.

From their devices, users may interact with their networks, publish updates, and check their social feeds. The apps offer a snappy and responsive experience because they are frequently tailored for mobile use.

Sharing and Connectivity: The Redmi Note 12 Pro 5G allows users to share content straight from other apps in addition to watching content from social media. Whether it's updating a status on social media or sending an email with a photo, the gadget puts seamless connectivity across various communication channels first.

Final Thought: A Coordinated Communication Environment

To sum up, the Redmi Note 12 Pro 5G positions itself as a center for integrated communication by providing consumers with a smooth and feature-rich messaging platform experience. The device accommodates a range of communication preferences, from standard text messaging to the various alternatives offered by messaging apps, including the integration of social media and email.

Improved communication is facilitated by user-centric features like read and delivery receipts, email push notifications, and messaging app security.

In a digital world where being in contact is crucial, the Redmi Note 12 Pro 5G offers more than just enable connection; it integrates the communication ecosystem. This guarantees that users stay effortlessly connected.

7. Internet and Connectivity

Smooth Access to the Digital World

Connectivity Profiles: The Redmi Note 12 Pro 5G might be compatible with a number of Bluetooth connectivity profiles, including Human Interface Device (HID) for attaching peripherals like keyboards and mice and Advanced Audio Distribution Profile (A2DP) for streaming high-quality audio. Because of its adaptability, users may connect their devices with ease and take advantage of a wide variety of wireless experiences.

Result: An Interconnected Way of Living

In conclusion, by offering consumers a strong internet and connectivity experience, the Redmi Note 12 Pro 5G epitomizes a connected lifestyle. The device guarantees that customers remain effortlessly connected to the digital world using various technologies, such as Bluetooth and NFC for ease and efficient Wi-Fi connections and optimal mobile data consumption.

The Redmi Note 12 Pro 5G places a premium on user-centric connectivity, whether it's for fast internet access, tracking mobile data usage, or easily connecting to peripherals.

The gadget becomes more than simply a tool for communication; it also becomes a friend that helps users move quickly, securely, and conveniently across the digital world.

8. Camera and Photography Expertise

Taking Precise Pictures

The Redmi Note 12 Pro 5G elevates the standard for mobile photography by offering consumers an advanced camera system that's meant to catch moments with originality and accuracy.

This section examines the device's entire camera experience, including how to use the Camera app, the craft of taking photos and videos, and the variety of camera settings and capabilities that allow users to embrace their inner photographers.

Using the Camera App: Simple Controls for Stress-Free Photography

The Redmi Note 12 Pro 5G's Camera app, which boasts simple controls for smooth shooting experiences, opens up a world of visual storytelling.

Accessible Launch: Redmi makes sure that users can easily and quickly access the Camera app by launching it from the home screen or lock screen with a single tap. The quick launch capability guarantees that customers may immediately film impromptu events.

User-Friendly Interface: The Camera app offers customers an intuitive interface with controls that are simple to use. Redmi usually arranges shooting modes, settings, and toggles in an easy-to-use and intuitive manner so that users can concentrate on crafting shots without then figuring out convoluted menus.

The Redmi Note 12 Pro 5G frequently comes with quick settings built right into the Camera app, enabling users to change things like exposure, white balance, and flash settings with only a few touches.

Furthermore, users can quickly transition between several shooting modes, guaranteeing versatility in capturing a range of situations.

Voice and Gesture Commands: The Camera app may allow voice and gesture commands for specific activities, adding an extra degree of convenience. To improve the hands-free shooting experience, users may utilize voice prompts or gestures to activate features like capturing a picture or alternating between the front and rear cameras.

Capturing Images and Videos: Accuracy in Each Frame

The Redmi Note 12 Pro 5G's camera skills are exceptional for both taking pictures and recording videos. Its ability to catch details in every shot allows users to express their ideas clearly and creatively through their images.

Excellent Photography: The gadget usually has a strong back camera configuration, frequently driven by high-megapixel sensors and cutting-edge optics. This guarantees clear, detailed images in a range of lighting scenarios. Pixel binning and multi-frame processing are two technologies Redmi might use to improve image quality, particularly in difficult circumstances.

Pro Mode for Photography Enthusiasts: The Redmi Note 12 Pro 5G offers a Pro mode that lets users manually adjust ISO, shutter speed, and focus, catering to those who love taking pictures.

This mode gives users the freedom to play around with various exposure settings, giving them a creative outlet.

AI-Powered Scene detection: The Camera app frequently has scene detection functions thanks to artificial intelligence. With its ability to recognize scenes and modify settings intelligently, the gadget maximizes the performance of the camera in a variety of situations, including low-light conditions, landscapes, and portraits.

Amazing Video Capabilities: The Redmi Note 12 Pro 5G boasts remarkable video capabilities that include superior stabilization technology and high-resolution filming.

4K resolution allows users to record cinematic moments, while features like electronic image stabilization (EIS) guarantee steady and fluid video even in fast-moving scenarios.

Features and Modes of the Camera: Unlocking Creativity

The Redmi Note 12 Pro 5G has an abundance of camera settings and features that enable users to express their creativity and capture a variety of viewpoints, going beyond the typical photo and video capture capabilities.

Night Mode for Low-Light Brilliance: One of the camera's most notable features, Night Mode allows users to take beautiful pictures in low light.

The Redmi Note 12 Pro 5G uses sophisticated algorithms to minimize noise and improve details, so nighttime photos have brightness and clarity.

Portrait Mode for Artistic Depth: Redmi usually comes with Portrait Mode, which enables users to take stunning photographs with exquisite depth of field. By cleverly identifying and separating the subject from the background, the gadget produces polished portraits with a blurred background.

Macro Photography for Up-close Detail: With a dedicated Macro mode, the Redmi Note 12 Pro 5G serves to photography aficionados who value the subtleties of the small world.

With the use of this mode, users may take incredibly close-up pictures that bring attention to textures and other elements that can be missed in more traditional photography.

Panorama and Pro Time-Lapse: Redmi's Panorama mode welcomes panoramic photography and lets users take expansive landscape photos in a single frame. The gadget might also have a Pro Time-Lapse mode that gives users exact control over interval settings to produce visually stunning time-lapse recordings.

AI Beauty and Filters for Expressive Shots: The Redmi Note 12 Pro 5G often comes with a range of filters and AI Beauty tools for users who like to add a creative touch to their images. With the help of these tools, users can add artistic filters, modify skin tones, and accentuate face characteristics to create unique and expressive photos.

Redefining Cellphone Photography

In conclusion, by providing users with an extensive and user-friendly camera experience, the Redmi Note 12 Pro 5G redefines mobile photography. The gadget puts the art of photography in the hands of its customers with its user-friendly controls, precise photo and video capture, and variety of creatively inspiring camera modes and functions.

The focus on cutting-edge technology, such as Night Mode and AI-powered scene identification, guarantees that users can take beautiful pictures under a range of circumstances.

With the Redmi Note 12 Pro 5G, users can express themselves through photography and record moments with unmatched creativity and precision. It's more than simply a smartphone.

9. Multimedia and Entertainment Excellence

The Redmi Note 12 Pro 5G is a multimedia powerhouse built to enhance digital experiences, not merely a communication tool.

We explore the device's gaming skills, music and video playing prowess, and smooth integration with streaming and content apps in this part, which offers customers an extensive and engaging entertainment environment.

Video Playback and Music: A Symphony of Sensual Pleasure

With its sophisticated multimedia features, the Redmi Note 12 Pro 5G creates a symphony of sensory delight for consumers as they enjoy music and videos.

Audio Excellence: When playing music, the gadget usually has high-quality audio components that provide a full-bodied and immersive sound experience. The Redmi Note 12 Pro 5G offers brilliant and clear audio, enhanced by a strong bass and well-defined highs, regardless of whether users prefer to stream their favorite songs or listen to locally saved music.

Dual Stereo Speakers: The Redmi Note 12 Pro 5G often has dual stereo speakers to improve the audio immersion. Users can experience a stereo effect thanks to its spatial audio configuration, which enhances the dynamic and captivating playback of music and videos. Whether held vertically or horizontally, the thoughtful positioning of the speakers enhances the overall audio experience.

Enhanced Video Playback: Users may enjoy their favorite films, TV series, and videos with clarity and detail thanks to the device's capability for high-resolution video playback. Redmi frequently adjusts video playback to maximize vibrant colors and striking contrasts, resulting in an amazing visual experience on the device's display.

Immersive Display Technologies: High refresh rates and support for HDR are two display technologies of the Redmi Note 12 Pro 5G that enhance the immersive entertainment experience. The gadget makes sure that every frame is a visual treat, whether users are enjoying smooth browsing and animations with a high refresh rate or watching HDR-enabled content for deeper colors and contrasts.

Redmi Note 12 Pro 5G Gaming: Energizing Play with Accuracy

The Redmi Note 12 Pro 5G is designed to satisfy the needs of mobile gamers by offering a precise and responsive gaming platform.

High-Performance   Processor:
Demanding games usually operate smoothly and without lag because the gadget usually has a high-performance processor. The Redmi Note 12 Pro 5G's chipset is built to withstand the strain, providing a fluid gaming experience regardless of the user's preference for graphically demanding or action-packed games.

Graphical and Display Optimization:
Redmi maximizes the graphical power of the smartphone for gaming, guaranteeing smooth frame rates and visually attractive games for players. The overall gaming visuals are improved with the incorporation of modern display technologies, such as adaptive refresh rate features and high

refresh rate, which make every swipe and action more responsive.

Game Turbo Mode: Redmi often comes with a special feature called Game Turbo mode, which maximizes system resources for a better gaming experience. In order to provide gamers a competitive edge during their gaming sessions, this mode might incorporate performance increases, wise resource usage, and cutting-edge gaming tools.

Cooling Technologies: The Redmi Note 12 Pro 5G frequently uses cutting-edge cooling technologies since it understands how important heat management is during prolonged gaming sessions.

In order to maintain gaming performance, this may incorporate liquid cooling systems or heat dissipation techniques that keep the device from overheating.

Apps for Content and Streaming: An Entrance to Endless Entertainment

With its smooth integration of streaming and multimedia apps, the Redmi Note 12 Pro 5G becomes a portal to an extensive entertainment collection.

Video Streaming Services: The Redmi Note 12 Pro 5G supports a variety of well-known video streaming services, allowing users to enjoy movies or binge-watch their favorite TV shows.

Apps like Netflix, Amazon Prime Video, and others are frequently pre-installed on the device, making it easy for users to access a wide variety of on-demand entertainment.

Music Streaming Platforms: Redmi supports the top music streaming platforms, allowing users to search, find, and enjoy their favorite music. The Redmi Note 12 Pro 5G delivers a flawless music streaming experience, whether you're making custom playlists, perusing carefully selected content, or taking advantage of high-definition audio streaming.

Smart Features and App Integration: The gadget frequently combines smart features from streaming apps, giving consumers a tailored and easy-to-use experience. capabilities like voice controls for playing content, user-preference-based content suggestions, and connection with smart home devices for a seamless entertainment ecosystem are possible capabilities that the Redmi Note 12 Pro 5G may support.

The Redmi Note 12 Pro 5G acknowledges the significance of social media and content creation in the digital sphere and offers apps for these purposes.

Users can easily share their multimedia works with others because of the device's smooth integration with social networking apps.

The Redmi Note 12 Pro 5G facilitates a wide range of content creation and sharing activities, including publishing stunning images on Instagram and making captivating short films on TikTok.

Final Thoughts: An Interactive Wonder

To sum up, the Redmi Note 12 Pro 5G is a multimedia marvel that redefines mobile entertainment. The gadget offers customers a holistic and immersive entertainment experience, from the symphony of audio perfection during music and movie playback to the accuracy and responsiveness in gaming and the smooth integration with streaming and content apps.

The Redmi Note 12 Pro 5G is more than just a smartphone; it's a multipurpose, portable entertainment center made to satiate a wide range of entertainment tastes.

The device guarantees that every digital experience is nothing short of amazing, whether users are exploring a world of on-demand content, immersing themselves in high-quality audio, or playing intensive games.

Redmi Note 12 Pro 5G

10. Battery and Charging Brilliance

Energizing Your Mobile Experience

The Redmi Note 12 Pro 5G is a technological marvel that shines in terms of battery management and quick charging in addition to its sophisticated features. This section covers the specifics of maximizing battery life with management advice and the effectiveness of the 67 Watt fast charger, making it possible for customers to quickly and dependably enhance their mobile experience.

Tips for Battery Management: Increasing Life and Effectiveness

Redmi Note 12 Pro 5G prioritizes effective battery management by giving consumers the tools and capabilities they need to extend battery life and improve overall performance.

Built-in battery optimization settings: Users can adjust their device's power consumption by utilizing the built-in battery optimization settings included on most devices. To help consumers balance performance and battery life, the Redmi Note 12 Pro 5G may come with power-saving settings, background app limits, and adaptive brightness capabilities.

App Usage Monitoring: Redmi frequently includes options to track how much time is spent on apps and how it affects battery life. Users are able to see comprehensive breakdowns of battery usage by specific apps, which gives them the ability to recognize and control power-hungry apps. The gadget might also provide recommendations for maximizing app settings to reduce power consumption.

Adaptive Battery Management: The Redmi Note 12 Pro 5G may make use of technologies that gradually learn user behavior in order to manage its battery. Based on usage patterns, the device dynamically modifies power allocation and background activities to optimize resources for the features and apps that users value.

Battery Health and Calibration: Redmi advises consumers to keep their batteries in good condition by avoiding extremely high or low temperatures and by calibrating them on a regular basis. The gadget might include battery health data, enabling customers to keep an eye on their battery's general condition and take preventative action to increase its lifespan.

67 Watt Charger for Quick Charging: Amazing Speeds of Power-Up

With its amazing 67 Watt fast charger, the Redmi Note 12 Pro 5G transforms the way people charge their smartphones and guarantees previously unheard-of speeds for customers to power up their devices.

Excellent Charging Speeds: One of the Redmi Note 12 Pro 5G's best features is its 67 Watt fast charger, which can provide excellent charging speeds. In just a few minutes, customers can observe a noticeable increase in their device's battery %, offering a prompt and effective solution for those leading hectic lives.

Quick Top-Ups for On-the-Go: The Redmi Note 12 Pro 5G's quick charging capabilities make it a perfect travel companion. The device makes sure that users can quickly top off their batteries, whether it's over a lunch break or a quick charge before going out for the evening.

Adaptive Charging Technologies: Redmi might use adaptive charging technologies, which adjust the charging process according to variables including usage habits and battery temperature. This promotes the general health of the battery by guaranteeing that the rapid charging procedure is not only quick but also effective and kind to the battery.

Charging Indicator and Notifications: To tell users of the charging status, the Redmi Note 12 Pro 5G normally has a charging indicator and notifications. The smartphone guarantees a transparent and easy-to-use charging experience, whether it's through real-time messages about charging completion or a visual signal on the lock screen.

Adding Power and Speed to Your Mobile Lifestyle

To sum up, the Redmi Note 12 Pro 5G is proof of the smooth fusion of state-of-the-art rapid charging and battery management technology. With its optimization settings and management recommendations, the gadget gives customers the ability to take charge of their battery life, assuring longevity and efficiency.

With the addition of the 67 Watt fast charger, consumers can now charge their gadgets at previously unheard-of speeds and have a quick and easy way to power them up.

In order to satisfy the needs of contemporary consumers, the Redmi Note 12 Pro 5G not only reinvents mobile technology but also embraces the spirit of a dynamic, connected lifestyle in which speed and power coexist.

With features like lightning-fast charging and battery life optimization, the smartphone makes sure customers can conveniently and confidently traverse their mobile experiences.

11. Settings and Customization Mastery

Along with its impressive hardware, the Redmi Note 12 Pro 5G gives customers access to a wide range of settings and customization possibilities.

This part explores the settings menu, app control features, and strong security and privacy aspects of the smartphone, emphasizing how users may precisely customize their digital experience.

System Preferences: Customizing the Device to Your Choices

With the wide selection of system settings that the Redmi Note 12 Pro 5G offers, users may tailor the smartphone to suit their tastes and usage habits.

Display and Brightness: Users can customize their visual experience by adjusting the display and brightness settings on the device. In order to fit their viewing tastes, users can explore options for color calibration, adjust the brightness of the screen, and enable adaptive brightness for automated adjustments based on environmental lighting.

Sound and Vibration: Redmi's sound and vibration settings provide customers complete control over their auditory experience. Users can personalize the device's auditory feedback by changing the notification and ringtone sounds, volume levels, and vibration strength settings.

Accessibility Features: To improve usability for all users, the Redmi Note 12 Pro 5G frequently integrates accessibility features into system settings. To ensure a more inclusive and customized experience, this may offer choices for motion controls, color inversion, and font size adjustments.

Language and Input: Users can adjust their preferred language under the system settings, and the device supports a wide range of languages. Users can select their favorite keyboard layout and input methods using the Redmi Note 12 Pro 5G's customizable keyboard choices.

Managing Applications: Optimizing Your Digital Environment

One of the main features of the Redmi Note 12 Pro 5G's user experience is its effective app management, which lets users arrange, customize, and optimize their digital ecosystem.

App Drawer and Home Screen Layout: For a customized and effective interface, Redmi often lets users alter the app drawer and home screen layout.

In order to fit their needs, users can rearrange icons, group programs into folders, and even change the grid arrangement.

App Permissions: By offering fine-grained control over app permissions, the device highlights user privacy. To maintain control over their data and personal information, users can select which apps have access to particular features or information.

App Notifications: The Redmi Note 12 Pro 5G has a feature-rich notification system that lets users tailor the settings for individual apps.

In accordance with their preferences, users can select notification tones, enable or disable particular app notifications, and even prioritize or silence notifications.

Automatic Downloads and App Updates: Usually, the device has settings for controlling downloads and updates for apps. For a smooth and current app experience, users can opt to enable automatic updates or update apps manually. Redmi minimizes interruptions by giving customers discretion over the timing and method of app updates.

Privacy and Security: Building Your Digital Stronghold

The Redmi Note 12 Pro 5G places a high priority on user security and privacy, providing a range of technologies that strengthen the device against possible security risks.

Face Unlock and Fingerprint Recognition: Redmi frequently uses sophisticated biometric authentication techniques like face unlock and fingerprint identification. The device can be unlocked using the user's preferred method, providing simple access and an additional degree of security.

App Lock and Secure Folders: Redmi offers features like app lock and secure folders in recognition of the need for extra app-specific security. Users can protect important data from unwanted access by locking specific programs or creating secure folders with improved security.

Privacy Settings: Users may manage the use and sharing of their data thanks to the device's extensive privacy settings. In order to improve their online privacy, users can investigate privacy options like Private DNS and adjust app permissions as well as location services.

Regular Software Updates with Security Patches: Redmi Note 12 Pro 5G gives security first priority when it comes to anti-malware measures.

In order to safeguard users' digital environments and to detect and block possible dangers, the device might additionally have anti-malware features.

Personalized Greatness Right at Your Fingertips

To sum up, the Redmi Note 12 Pro 5G is a shining example of customized brilliance, providing consumers with an abundance of settings and customisable options to improve their digital life.

The gadget puts personalization and control at the fingertips of consumers, whether it's reinforcing security and privacy, personalizing the display, or managing the app ecosystem.

The Redmi Note 12 Pro 5G offers consumers more than just a smartphone; it's a blank canvas on which to precisely customize their digital lives.

The device makes sure that users have the tools to customize their digital experience to their preferences, from the system settings that determine how the device behaves to the app management features that simplify the user interface and the strong security and privacy measures that bolster the digital fortress.

Customization is more than just a feature in the Redmi Note 12 Pro 5G universe; it's a mindset that enables customers to genuinely personalize their device.

12. Troubleshooting and Support

Choosing Smooth Solutions

The Redmi Note 12 Pro 5G is not immune to glitches, as even the most sophisticated gadgets can have them.

In order to guarantee a dependable and seamless user experience, this part discusses the extensive customer service resources as well as addressing frequent issues that users may run into.

Common Problems and Their Fixes: A Handbook for Smooth Settlements

Although Redmi Note 12 Pro 5G aims to give users a trouble-free experience, problems can occasionally occur. This is a list of typical issues and possible fixes:

1. Battery Drain: Look for background programs that are using up power if you observe an excessive amount of battery drain. To maximize battery life, close any unused programs, change settings, and look for software updates that might address power management.

2. Connectivity Issues: Turn the corresponding connection on and off to begin troubleshooting Bluetooth, Wi-Fi, or mobile data. Make sure that your device is in range of the network or device you are attempting to connect to, and that airplane mode is turned off. Connectivity problems may also be fixed by upgrading firmware or resetting network configurations.

3. App Crashes: Make sure certain apps are updated to the most recent version if you notice that they are crashing. If the problem continues, try cleaning the app's cache and reinstalling the affected version. It could be necessary to do a system update if numerous apps are impacted.

4. Performance Lag: You can improve slow performance by making sure you have enough storage space, shutting off background apps, and tweaking system settings. Check for program upgrades, since they frequently feature performance improvements, if performance problems continue.

5. Display Issues: Make sure that the screen brightness settings are set correctly to address display-related problems. whether the issue continues, see whether there are any updates available. Frequently, software upgrades address issues relating to displays. In severe circumstances, a factory reset or seeing a specialist can be necessary.

6. Camera Malfunctions: Try closing and restarting the Camera app if the camera isn't working properly. Make sure there are no dirt or obstructions on the camera lens. Check for software upgrades or think about contacting customer support for more help if the problem continues.

7. Software Glitches: Restarting the device will fix any unexpected software issues. Should the issue continue, it might be essential to look for software updates or carry out a factory reset in order to address any underlying software problems.

Redmi Users' Lifeline: Customer Support Resources

Users of the Redmi Note 12 Pro 5G have access to a wealth of customer care services, so help is always close at hand when they need it.

1. Official Website Support part: Users may find FAQs, troubleshooting manuals, and other support materials in the dedicated support part of the official Redmi website. This online resource is a helpful place for consumers to start when looking for answers to frequent problems.

2. Online Community Forums: Redmi has active online community forums where users may interact and exchange tips with other Redmi fans.

Community forums frequently offer insightful conversations, user-generated troubleshooting manuals, and solutions to specific issues.

3. Customer service Hotline: Redmi offers customer service hotlines so that customers can get in touch with support representatives directly. Trained support staff that can walk users through troubleshooting procedures, provide information on software updates, and provide solutions for frequent issues staff these hotlines.

4. Service Centers: Redmi offers in-person assistance for more difficult issues at its service centers, which are spread around different areas.

These facilities frequently feature diagnostic equipment and skilled technicians on hand to handle hardware-related issues and carry out repairs as needed.

5. Social Media Channels: Users can interact with Redmi on more platforms by visiting its official social media accounts on Facebook and Twitter. These channels frequently address user questions and concerns, announce software changes, and offer updates on recognized problems.

6. Email Support: Customers can frequently email Redmi's support staff with their complaints, accompanied by a written communication. Email assistance is especially helpful for complex questions or problems that can take longer to resolve.

7. User Manuals and Documentation:

The online documentation and user manual for the item are helpful tools for troubleshooting and comprehending its functionality. These resources can be consulted by users seeking detailed instructions and explanations of particular features.

Final Thought: Providing Users with Helpful Solutions

To sum up, assistance and troubleshooting for the Redmi Note 12 Pro 5G are essential parts of the user experience. Redmi is dedicated to giving users quick access to helpful tools so they can easily browse and take care of frequent problems.

Redmi makes sure that consumers have a lifeline to solve issues as soon as they arise, whether it's a speedy fix through online tutorials, the combined knowledge of community forums, direct assistance via customer support hotlines, or in-person support at service centers.

In addition to fixing problems, the troubleshooting and support ecosystem provides consumers with the information and help they need to get the most out of their Redmi Note 12 Pro 5G experience.

13. Accessories and Extra Features

Improving the Experience of Your Redmi Note 12 Pro 5G

Along with its impressive performance and stylish appearance, the Redmi Note 12 Pro 5G is distinguished by the variety of accessories that can be added to improve and personalize the user experience.

This section dives into the unique characteristics that set the Redmi Note 12 Pro 5G apart from other devices in its category and examines the suitable accessories that are made for it.

Suggested Add-ons: Enhancing Usability and Design

Redmi guarantees that a variety of compatible accessories that satisfy both functionality and appearance may be used by consumers to enhance their Redmi Note 12 Pro 5G experience.

1. Protective Cases and Covers: Redmi provides a range of covers and cases designed specifically to safeguard the Redmi Note 12 Pro 5G. These add-ons not only shield the device from normal wear and tear but also give it a customized look. A variety of materials are available for users to select from, such as sturdy protective cases and fashionable covers for a more aesthetically pleasing look.

2. Screen Protectors: Redmi offers compatible screen protectors that are made to withstand scratches and small knocks in order to protect the device's display. These translucent layers provide an extra line of protection against common dangers while guaranteeing that the touch screen stays responsive.

3. Chargers and Cables: Although the Redmi Note 12 Pro 5G frequently ships with a fast charger, customers may want to purchase extra chargers and cables to make their lives easier when they're in different places. Redmi guarantees that a variety of charging accessories, such as power banks and auto chargers, are compatible, enabling customers to maintain their battery levels while on the go.

4. Wireless Earbuds and Headphones:
Redmi Note 12 Pro 5G owners can improve their music enjoyment by using earbuds and headphones that work with the device. Redmi provides a range of hands-free calling, immersive gaming, and wireless audio accessories that interface with the device in an easy-to-use manner to eliminate tangles.

5. Fitness Bands and Smartwatches:
Redmi offers fitness bands and smartwatches that are compatible for customers who want to track their health and fitness stats.

Users can effortlessly track their physical activity, receive notifications, and stay connected while on the go with these accessories that sync with the Redmi Note 12 Pro 5G.

6. Camera Accessory: To improve their experience with mobile photography, photography enthusiasts might investigate appropriate camera accessories. This might include tripods, clip-on lenses, and other add-ons made to enhance the artistic potential of the remarkable camera system on the Redmi Note 12 Pro 5G.

7. Gaming Controllers: Because of the Redmi Note 12 Pro 5G's powerful gaming capabilities, users can choose to improve their gaming experience by using compatible game controllers. By providing accurate controls and tactile feedback, these controllers transform the tablet into a portable gaming console.

Redmi Note 12 Pro 5G's Unique Features: Setting It Apart

In addition to being accessory compatible, the Redmi Note 12 Pro 5G has a number of unique features that set it apart from competing smartphones.

1. 5G Connectivity: The Redmi Note 12 Pro 5G, as its name implies, has 5G connectivity, which enables users to enjoy extremely high internet speeds and minimal latency.

This makes the device future-proof for changing network technologies and guarantees a flawless experience for streaming, gaming, and other data-intensive operations.

2. Excellent Camera System: The camera system of the Redmi Note 12 Pro 5G is quite remarkable. High-megapixel sensors, sophisticated optics, and a range of camera modes guarantee that users can take beautiful pictures and videos in a variety of situations. The camera system is a major standout for low-light and detailed macro photography.

3. High-Refresh-Rate Display: The Note 12 Pro 5G from Redmi frequently has a high-refresh-rate display, which offers consumers responsive touch interactions and better animations. When it comes to social media scrolling, gaming, or video watching, a fast refresh rate makes the user experience smoother and more pleasurable.

4. Fast Processor: To provide quick performance and seamless multitasking, the gadget usually has a fast processor, like the MediaTek Dimensity 1080. From managing resource-intensive apps and games to navigating the UI, this potent chipset improves the user experience overall.

5. Large Battery Capacity: The Redmi Note 12 Pro 5G has a large battery capacity, typically around 5000mAh, so users won't have to worry about running out of power during the course of the day.

When coupled with effective power management, the device's substantial battery capacity adds lifespan.

6. Stereo Speakers: The Redmi Note 12 Pro 5G might have stereo speakers to provide a rich audio experience. With clear and dynamic sound for watching movies, playing games, or listening to music, this spatial audio system improves consumers' multimedia consumption.

7. Vibrant Display Technology: Redmi frequently incorporates technology for vibrant displays, like vivid color reproduction and support for HDR.

This guarantees that viewers, whether they are looking at pictures, watching films, or playing games, will have an aesthetically spectacular and engaging experience.

A Whole Mobile Experience

To sum up, the Redmi Note 12 Pro 5G offers consumers a whole mobile experience with a variety of compatible accessories and exceptional capabilities, going beyond just being a smartphone.

Redmi makes sure there are accessories to suit consumers' demands, whether they want to secure their device, improve their music experience, or experiment with photography for artistic purposes.

The Redmi Note 12 Pro 5G stands out in its category thanks to its unique features, which include 5G connection, a potent camera system, and a high-refresh-rate display.

For those looking for a complete and satisfying mobile experience, the Redmi Note 12 Pro 5G is a versatile and intriguing option thanks to its unique features and well-considered accessories.

14. Safety and Regulation Information

Redmi Note 12 Pro 5G Puts User Well-Being First

Redmi places a high priority on user safety and wellbeing, and the Redmi Note 12 Pro 5G is no different.

This part offers a thorough examination of the regulatory compliance procedures built into the device as well as the crucial safety considerations that users should follow.

Critical Safety Measures: Handling the Device Carefully

Redmi stresses the value of user safety and offers thorough instructions to make sure users can use the Redmi Note 12 Pro 5G in a secure manner. The following are important safety measures that consumers need to know:

1. Battery Handling: The lithium-ion battery that powers the Redmi Note 12 Pro 5G should be handled carefully; users should adhere to certain instructions. This includes staying out of direct sunlight, shielding the battery from physical harm, and not trying to disassemble the gadget.

2. Charger Usage: Redmi advises utilizing only approved chargers and cords and offers detailed instructions for using the provided charger. It is advised against using third-party or damaged charging accessories by users as they could be dangerous.

3. Device Placement: It is suggested that users keep the Redmi Note 12 Pro 5G out of direct sunlight and heat sources to prevent excessive heat from affecting the device's battery life and performance. To further avoid any damage, the device should be kept in a dry, cool environment.

4. Water and Dust Resistance: Users should be aware of the Redmi Note 12 Pro 5G's unique IP classification and limitations, even though the device may offer water and dust resistance to some level.

It is imperative that the gadget not be submerged in water for longer than its rated depth.

5. Correct Cleaning: Redmi offers instructions on how to clean the gadget properly, suggesting that users wipe the screen and body with a gentle, lint-free cloth. The surfaces of the gadget should not be harmed by abrasive materials or harsh chemicals.

6. Emergency Calls: Redmi stresses how crucial it is to know how to use the device's emergency call functionality. Even when the device is locked, users should know how to make emergency calls to guarantee prompt aid in dire circumstances.

7. Usage in Hazardous Environments:
When utilizing the Redmi Note 12 Pro 5G in potentially dangerous settings, such as places with flammable materials or explosive atmospheres, users should proceed with caution. In order to avoid any possible safety issues, the device should be turned off in certain types of circumstances.

Regulatory Conformity: Upholding International Guidelines

In order to reinforce the Redmi Note 12 Pro 5G's safety and compliance with international legislation, Redmi makes sure the gadget conforms with regulatory standards and certifications.

1. FCC Compliance: To guarantee that electronic devices do not create detrimental interference, the Federal Communications Commission (FCC) establishes rules. In order for the Redmi Note 12 Pro 5G to be lawfully marketed and used in the United States, it must pass stringent testing and certification procedures that are required by the FCC.

2. CE Marking: The European Union (EU) safety standards are indicated by the CE marking, a certification mark. In order for the Redmi Note 12 Pro 5G to be sold and promoted lawfully inside the European Economic Area (EEA), Redmi makes sure that it complies with certain regulations.

3. RoHS Compliance: Certain hazardous compounds cannot be used in electronic or electrical equipment, according to the Restriction of Hazardous Substances (RoHS) directive. Redmi guarantees that the Redmi Note 12 Pro 5G complies with RoHS regulations, encouraging ethical production practices and environmental safety.

4. Industry Canada Certification: In order to comply with Canadian regulations, Industry Canada certifies the Redmi Note 12 Pro 5G. By doing this, the gadget's electromagnetic compatibility and radiofrequency exposure are guaranteed to meet Canadian regulations.

5. CCC Certification: To guarantee the safety of products, China has implemented a statutory certification system called the China Compulsory Certificate (CCC). Redmi makes sure the Redmi Note 12 Pro 5G is CCC certified, which enables it to be used and sold lawfully in China.

6. Other Regional Certifications: To guarantee that the Redmi Note 12 Pro 5G complies with regional laws and safety criteria, Redmi maintains a number of extra regional certifications and standards. This comprises approvals from authorities in charge of regulations in the many nations and areas where the gadget is marketed.

Acknowledgment of User Responsibility and Regulatory Compliance: A Joint Effort

Redmi promotes a cooperative approach to safety by highlighting the mutual accountability of the user and the maker. When configuring and using the Redmi Note 12 Pro 5G, users are usually obliged to recognize and embrace the significance of abiding by safety regulations and legal requirements.

Users may come across safety information and compliance acknowledgments throughout the device setup process, which calls on them to verify that they understand safety precautions and regulatory compliance.

This cooperative strategy guarantees that users are aware of the device's safety features and are dedicated to using it in a way that complies with international regulations.

Final Thoughts: Guaranteeing a Safe and Legal Environment

In conclusion, Redmi's dedication to giving customers a safe and compliant experience is demonstrated by the safety and regulatory facts around the Redmi Note 12 Pro 5G mobile encounter. Redmi provides comprehensive safety measures and complies with international regulations to guarantee that the Redmi Note 12 Pro 5G is safe and legal in many regions while also putting the needs of its users first.

With the Redmi Note 12 Pro 5G, users may interact with the gadget with confidence because it is safe to use and conforms with international regulatory frameworks. The Redmi Note 12 Pro 5G is a safe and pleasurable device to use, thanks to users and Redmi working together to follow safety recommendations.

More than simply a smartphone, the Redmi Note 12 Pro 5G offers a doorway to the wide world of the internet and seamless connectivity. This section examines the ways in which the device empowers consumers through Bluetooth and NFC conveniences, efficient mobile data utilization, and Wi-Fi connectivity.

Wi-Fi Link: Building a Bridge to Fast Internet

The Redmi Note 12 Pro 5G prioritizes Wi-Fi connectivity, providing customers with fast internet access for a range of uses.

Wi-Fi Configuration: Most devices have an easy-to-use Wi-Fi configuration process that makes it simple for users to connect to available networks. Redmi simplifies the setup process by assisting consumers in choosing a network, providing a password if necessary, and connecting with a few taps.

Wi-Fi Optimization: Redmi frequently includes capabilities for Wi-Fi optimization in order to improve performance.

This might involve clever network switching, in which the gadget switches between mobile data and Wi-Fi without a hitch to keep a steady connection. Furthermore, the device may select well-known and reliable Wi-Fi networks as the default connection point.

Wi-Fi Security Features: The Redmi Note 12 Pro 5G supports the most recent Wi-Fi security protocols since it understands how important security is for wireless communications. WPA3-secured networks are accessible to users, guaranteeing a safe environment for data transfer and guarding against security flaws.

Mobile Data Usage: Encouraging Mobility and Connectivity

Redmi Note 12 Pro 5G optimizes mobile data usage for customers who are constantly on the go, guaranteeing a dependable and effective internet connection no matter where they go.

Data Usage Monitoring: Redmi usually comes with an extensive data usage monitoring tool that lets customers check how much data they consume on their mobile devices. With the help of this function, users may monitor comprehensive data usage breakdowns by app, establish data usage limitations, and receive alerts when they are about to exceed their allotted data.

Data Saver option: The Redmi Note 12 Pro 5G may come with a Data Saver option to save mobile data and prolong battery life. When enabled, this option limits the amount of background data that apps can use. This way, data is only used for important tasks and front apps, cutting down on needless background data usage.

5G Connectivity: The Redmi Note 12 Pro 5G is outfitted to take use of 5G connectivity, as suggested by its moniker. This cutting-edge technology guarantees reduced latency, quicker upload and download times, and a more responsive online experience.

Depending on the user's requirements and the available network infrastructure, the device dynamically transitions between 5G and other network modes to maximize connectivity.

NFC and Bluetooth: Integrated Short-Range Communication

With Bluetooth and NFC technologies, the Redmi Note 12 Pro 5G offers consumers seamless short-range alternatives that improve communication beyond internet access.

Bluetooth Connectivity: The device's Bluetooth technology allows users to establish wireless connections with a variety of accessories, such as speakers, headphones, smartwatches, and more. Redmi makes pairing simple, making it easy for consumers to connect to other devices that are compatible. The device's Bluetooth is usually energy-efficiently tuned to minimize the impact on battery life when connecting wirelessly.

NFC (Near Field Communication): The Redmi Note 12 Pro 5G often features NFC technology for speedy and secure interactions. This lets users connect with other NFC-enabled devices, share files, and start transactions by only bringing their devices close to one another. Convenience is increased by NFC on the smartphone, particularly when using it for mobile payments and device pairing.